MW01274769

Our
Children

Common Sense
Parenting
in a
Complex World

~ ⊗ ~

Jill Turnbull

Publishing-Partner

Publishing-Partners
Port Townsend, WA
www.publishing-partners.com
info@publishing-partners.com

© 2015 Jill Turnbull All rights reserved.
jillturnbull@yahoo.com

ISBN: 978-0-9862830-4-8

Library of Congress Control Number: 2015946129

Printed in the United States of America
10 9 8 7 6 5 4 3 2 1

Editor: Sherilynn Gold
Typographer: Marcia Breece
Cover: Marcia Breece

Contents

Dedication

I dedicate this book to

My beloved children,

Arielle & Yuri

And their father, Ken

Of all the things I have done,

Motherhood has brought me the greatest joy.

Acknowledgements

Thank you to my typists: Arielle, Yuri, Kimberly Absher, Marcia Breece, Jill LaRue.

Editor Sherilynn Gold.

Thank you to my wonderful network of friends who love and support me unconditionally; without you, I'd be lost. Lorraine, Jill LaRue, Marianne, Leslie, Lynnji, Supriya, Ursula, Alima, Suguna & Theo.

Arielle & Yuri, you are the best kids any mother could ask for. How I cherish you. I know you truly care about my happiness, what a gift.

Prologue

Dear Parents,

The purpose of this book is to help you navigate through the ups and downs, the twists and turns and the challenges of parenting; certainly one of life's most difficult jobs. Let's face it, as new parents, we're all just winging it. Let's add wisdom to the flight.

How many times have I heard parents joke and lament that there is no instruction manual for raising kids? God knows, there are countless manuals out there for far less important things. Raising children is the most important job on the planet and, I believe, the most challenging.

This book was born out of my concern for our youth, who are growing up in turbulent times. Values are out of whack and there's too much violence, apathy, materialism and stress. Many kids are looking lost, disheveled and glued to one screen or another. Yes, looks can be deceiving, but I believe that the youth of today are off track. Society's values are leading many of our next generation away from some of the very positive things *we* valued and that make for strong, caring adults. Kids are the future and our most valuable resource. The responsibility for the world will soon be in their hands. What kind of leaders are we producing?

In this book, I share with you the knowledge I have gleaned from having raised my two children. My hope is that by reading it, you will get some helpful ideas in your quest to produce happy, healthy kids and families.

We all desire to raise wonderful, independent, generous children who will one day leave the nest and fly into their adult lives ready to take on the life that awaits them. May this book help you with that process.

I think it is important to note that none of us are perfect. We do our best with the situation we are in and must learn to forgive ourselves when we err. You may not agree with me completely, but I know there is something here for all readers, new ideas to entertain and consider. Try to keep an open mind and think outside the box. The more creative your thinking, the more parenting can be an enjoyable, interesting journey and yield creative, intelligent and broad-minded children.

I have purposefully kept this book short because parents are too busy to read reams of material and I do not wish to replicate what has already been written.

Good luck and Godspeed.

Chapter One

Love Is All That Really Matters

*If you love someone, the greatest gift you
can give them is your presence.*
—Thich Nhat Hanh

I do not think enough can be said about both
parents showing their children how much they
love and cherish them. Hugging and kissing your
children, no matter their age or gender, is crucial, as
well as saying the words "I love you, I'm glad you're
my child" and (when appropriate), "I'm proud of
you". I have even said, "There is nothing you can do
that will ever turn me away from you".

Hold them, touch them, kiss them, generally
be affectionate with them. They will learn to love
themselves if they feel loved by you, and they cannot
get the feeling of being attractive unless they actually
experience it with *you*, the most important person
in their young lives. "Being touched and held by a
parent is crucial in the development of a young child's
self-image."[1] "When a child grows up to love himself,
to be self-confident, to have high self-esteem, and to
respect himself, there are literally no obstacles to his
total fulfilment as a human being."[2]

There is so much estrangement and isolation in
our society; let there be love and a sense of belonging

in your home. A safe haven is an oasis in a stressful world. Try to keep peace and harmony in your home.

It is said that the most precious gift one can give another is their time. Try to find some time every day to check in with and *listen* to your children. With older kids, bedtime seems to be the ideal time for this (though it is not usually our ideal time).

Try to spend pleasant time together as family, whether it's once a week or once a month. This solidifies your relationships and makes for nice memories. Also, let your kids see you and your partner being affectionate with each other.

It is hard to be a child. Accepting who your child is, at their core, is crucial. They are not clones. We all wish to be accepted for who we are and usually resent those who try to change us. Convey that you are proud of your child for who he is as a person, not for what he does. There is a big difference. Say, "I love that you have a big heart" or "I love that you are generous and caring", whatever is true for you. Tune into who the child is and enforce his good qualities. Expressions of love and caring help children to know that they are not alone; they are supported and cared about.

Reading to your child is an act of love and an opportunity to bond. I have fond memories of my mother reading *Heidi* to my sister and me. I am seeing more and more moms on their cell phones while out walking with their children or supervising them at parks or beaches. I *urge* you to put the phone away and spend this *precious* time engaged with your children. Talk and laugh with them, sing to them; even babies enjoy our attention while they are being pushed in the stroller. This precious time of total dependence will pass quickly, cherish it.

Time seems to speed up as children get older. I would give just about anything for a week with my tiny children!

* * * * *

Chapter Two

Enjoying Life/Happiness

The greatest gift you can ever give your children
is to be an example of happiness.
—**Author unknown**

Wouldn't we all like our children to have the ability to enjoy life? If at all possible, try to model enjoying life enthusiastically so your children see your example and follow it. Children learn by watching us. Try to carve out time for doing the things you love and are passionate about. Let your children see you doing these things or tell them what you are doing and why. Perhaps it's getting out in nature, photography, visiting museums, reading, horseback riding, dancing, drawing, playing music or cooking. As Joseph Cornell said, "Nothing is so contagious as enthusiasm."

Assess your strengths and feel good about them. Each of us is good at something and we can brighten the world with our "gifts". Give of yourself freely. *Help your children discover their gifts and passions* and then support them wholeheartedly. We are here on earth to discover our true inner selves and higher purpose. We are here to be of service and to make the world a better place. We are here to love one another and live our passion, whatever that is for each of us and to find *JOY*. May you find your purpose and your joy and be an inspiration to your offspring to find theirs.

Grow your happiness through positive interactions. I notice that the more I think of other's happiness and ways to brighten someone else's day, the better I feel and the more I enjoy my day. Share your smile with someone, anyone, and notice how good it feels, even if they do not respond.

Happiness is inside of us and can be "triggered" by feelings of gratitude. There is always something to be grateful for. It could be as simple as having gotten a good nights' sleep, it's a sunny day, having a roof over our heads, knowing someone cares about us, having reliable transportation, food in the fridge, clothes, a job… we are (indeed) alive, our child is healthy. If we can remember to be grateful for our blessings once a day or even several times a day, it "colors" the day, and feelings of happiness and contentment will follow. *Teach your children to count their blessings every day.*

This may sound odd, but when I keep the corners of my mouth turned up, I feel uplifted! Chemicals associated with happiness are released in the brain when we smile, even if it is (at first) a forced smile. Try it! We can choose to "live as though nothing is a miracle or live as though everything is![3]" After all, *Happiness is our birthright and it is a choice.*

In our culture we are programmed to think that accumulating things makes us happy. The truth is that accumulating things of any kind brings only momentary pleasure. Many people, if not most, are imprisoned in the past or the future. The only thing that we can "possess" is the here and now. So, *be here now,* in this very moment, and experience the joy that brings.

"Don't postpone joy"
—Bumper sticker

*   *   *   *   *

Chapter Three

Kindness

Educating the mind without educating the heart,
is no education at all.
—**Aristotle**

*K*indness is often forgotten these days. Take a moment to say or do something kind for your child, such as, "You have a lovely smile." Or, "You look cold; I'll bring you a sweater. Would you like a hot drink?" Smile at your child with your mouth and your eyes.

Model kindness for your child by treating everyone in your world as if they are special to you. If we would just "Do unto others...." we could heal the planet! It feels good inside to be loving and compassionate. Try to be aware that we all struggle with challenges of one kind or another. You may be looking at someone whose father has just died, or someone who was just told they have cancer. Let your children see you helping others, even if it is just seeing you smile at people as you shop and asking them how they are, or holding a door for someone. Explain to your child later why you are kind to strangers.

Nowadays I hear kids "dissing" each other. Please do not allow this; it can become a negative habit and be hurtful to the recipient. The same with bullying, it must be stopped immediately and reported no matter whose child it is. Insist that your children treat everyone they come in contact with kindly, including you, their siblings, friends, and others.

It is hard to be a child. When they go through difficult times, you do not need to try to fix things. Validating their feelings goes a long way. Respond as you would with a friend, saying, "That must be hard for you" or "That must have been embarrassing." It is appropriate to ask them if they would like some ideas on how to resolve difficult situations. This lets the child know he is not alone, stumbling around in the dark. These responses will also do wonders for your relationship if you are married or partnered. We all desire and deserve to be treated with kindness and caring.

Please don't talk about your child in front of her, no matter how young. It makes her feel like an object and she has ears!

Commit to working out differences with your partner kindly and strive to keep peace and harmony in the home. Children need to see parents treating each other respectfully so they learn how to treat their future partners. This is extremely crucial if parents are separating or divorcing. Please, don't degrade your ex in front of your child. Children need to respect their parents, whether you do or not.

Parents, being kind to ourselves during these challenging years helps us feel more loving with our children. Nurture yourselves throughout the day with little rests or breaks. Let the children observe you taking care of yourself.

Please apologize for your mistakes. It lets children know that no one is perfect; we all have difficult moments and perhaps do things we later regret.

If you don't live with your children, please find it in your heart to stay involved in their lives. This is crucial to a child's feeling of self-worth. Staying involved is a win-win as both you and the children benefit tremendously. You will feel good about yourself and everyone's life will be enriched.

Try to stay on good terms with all the people in your life; this brings peace of mind. We're all wounded in one way or another and are all doing the best we can. Forgive people their faults and shortcomings and try not to take things personally. Offer your smile to all who cross your path and know that your good cheer will radiate out into the world.

＊　＊　＊　＊　＊

Chapter Four

Taking Care of Ourselves

There is more to life than increasing its speed.
—Mahatma Gandhi

Nurture yourself throughout the day when you can. If the baby is sleeping, take a nap too. If the child is happily playing, sit down with a cup of tea and rest for a few minutes. Put on nice music. Have a sitter come over for an hour while you take a relaxing bath. Take time out for yourself and with your partner if you have one. Get out of the house now and then for a meal out, a movie, a walk. Have someone take over watching the kids so you can do something you really enjoy. Err on the side of getting more sleep vs. a clean house! The dust and dishes can wait. You will be more patient and loving if you are rested.

A babysitting co-op was a godsend for my family. This is a group of like-minded parents who agree to care for each other's children as needed and for breaks. I joined an existing group of about six families and we grew to twelve. We used a point system; one point earned for each hour of babysitting. Adult and child friendships developed and we all felt more comfortable leaving our children with other parents rather than with teenagers just out to earn spending money. I felt comfortable going on a date with my husband knowing my children were in good hands and having fun playing with the sitter's children. As a group, we even had our own Halloween parties because we did not want the kids eating tons of candy. The co-op was truly a win-win situation for everyone involved. You can start a co-op with just one other family and keep adding on. Heaven knows, we can all use help from like-minded people.

Parenting is challenging and children can be exasperating. Frustration and angry feelings will be felt from time to time. We all feel these strong emotions periodically. It is normal, we are human. What is crucial is how we deal with the feelings. If we do not feed them they will dissipate. It is our own internal frustration that causes us to want to yell and expel pent-up emotions. But as adults we must find healthy ways to deal with frustration. The best ways allow us to both take care of ourselves and preserve our relationships.

Take deep breaths (many), leave the room, pound the bed, get on the treadmill, shake out a rug, run around the block or call a friend. But *please* preserve your relationship with your child AND model being a kind, in-control adult who does not yell. It is perfectly okay to tell the child that you are getting grouchy and need a break. THEN TAKE ONE.

* * * * *

Chapter Five

Holidays & Celebrations

You have to give to receive.

If you have young children, this is the perfect time to give some thought to how you and your family desires to celebrate special occasions. Young families can change some of the traditions that really do not make sense. In this culture I feel that too much emphasis is placed on lavishing children with gifts. Once you start doing that, children expect it every year.

Excessive gift giving (materialism at its best) does not send the right message. Yes, it is nice to receive things, and one or two thoughtful gifts, carefully considered, coupled with love and quality time spent together, can express as much caring, if not more, than too many gifts given without much thought.

If you already have a big gift giving routine going, i.e. for Christmas, and desire to change it, the kids may be disappointed. However, children are resilient. They will adjust to the change if you explain why and substitute something else, for instance taking them on a special outing. You might even make personalized gift certificates inviting your children on a "date" to the aquarium or to the zoo, an amusement park, picnic, a special play or concert, dinner and a movie, a ski trip. Special time with Mom or Dad is extremely important to children. They want it and need it and may remember these occasions for the rest of their lives. My father took me to breakfast when I was about ten years old. I still remember it fondly. Such a little thing in the eyes of an adult, but as a child I was delighted.

Spouses can also give each other gift certificates such as for a professional massage or one given by them. You might get creative and ask the members of your family to make gifts for each other for a year and see how successful it is. Purchasing gifts from thrift stores can be fun too, and is a nice way to teach children about reusing resources, saving money and helping the earth. Many thrift stores have very interesting and inexpensive items.

In our family, when the kids were young, we celebrated birthdays by inviting their friends over and playing games in the backyard or at a nearby park. When they got older, we rented the swimming pool at the local recreation center, then came home for the healthy cake I made.

There are countless ways to celebrate birthdays. Little girls might like to invite their friends and mothers to dress up and come over for a tea party. I personally think gratitude circles are lovely at parties. Everyone takes turns saying what they like about each other or what they are grateful for. As for food, why do we feel the need to eat sugar-laden cake to welcome in a new year? I think serving the birthday child's favorite meal for dinner, then doing something special with her that she enjoys is a much better idea.

*   *   *   *   *

Chapter Six

The Great Outdoors

We do not inherit the Earth from our ancestors;
we borrow it from our children.
—Chief Seattle

When I think back to my childhood, what I remember most are all the wonderful times spent playing outside. Riding bikes, climbing trees, running for the sheer joy of it, swimming, and playing games with friends and my sister.

Studies show that children now spend 93% of their time indoors, often involving long hours in front of one type of screen or another. The term "nature-deficit disorder" has been coined as a result of this phenomenon. According to Richard Louv, author of the best-selling book *Last Child in the Woods: Saving Our Children From Nature-Deficit Disorder*, there are negative health effects on individuals and their communities when a connection with nature isn't present in young people. Furthermore he says, "The children and nature movement is fueled by this fundamental idea: the child in nature is an endangered species, and the health of children and the health of the Earth are inseparable."

I encourage you to get outside with your children, no matter what the weather is like. Breathe deeply (if the air is reasonably clean), watch the animals and birds, romp, shoot hoops, watch the grass grow or the cloud formations. Garden. Day dream. Chill out. Somehow the stresses of life seem to melt away.

When it's cold outside, bundle up. If it's rainy, don rain gear and umbrellas. Kids love holding umbrellas and splashing through puddles. They're only young once, let them have fun and get dirty; they'll stay reasonably warm and dry. It's worth the time and effort to let them explore their world and come to cherish it. My twenty-eight year old daughter still thrills at the sight of snow!

Adults are the models; when children see you outside enjoying yourselves, they are more likely to want to do the same throughout their lives and they will be healthier for it.

Let your children run around and get rid of pent up energy after a long car ride or after being in school all day. This is especially good to do before going somewhere where they need to be quiet and well behaved. Walk, drive or bike to a park and let them RUN.

If your child's school is eliminating recess, speak up *loudly* (but politely) and try to bring it back. Get other parents to help you. Kids need a break from learning; they need exercise and to socialize in ways that are different when they are on the playground.

*   *   *   *   *

Chapter Seven

Entertainment/Play

A child is not a vase to be filled, but a fire to be lit.
—Francois Rabelais

Boredom is a choice. Out of boredom comes creativity. Allow children to be bored some of the time and they will invent interesting games, draw pictures, write stories and contemplate their future. Build in time for day dreaming and watching cloud formations.

Encourage kids to make some of their own toys, the more the better. Allow them to play with pots and pans, soap and water, mud in a puddle. They can dress up their dolls and stuffed animals and serve them the tea and cookies they make. You can make your own play-dough (my grandmother made it with flour, salt and water). Kids love to build forts and hideaways with blankets hung over chairs. They can write and perform plays. Little children can dictate a story or a play to you if they can't yet write. These can be saved as they are precious treasures. Slow the pace. Life is not a race or a contest to see how much we can fit into a day.

Two children together can come up with all sorts of ideas for how to spend an afternoon. Encourage friendships; invite friends over, yours and theirs. Let the children make their own lunch and wash the dishes. *Encourage reading* and looking at books. Let them see you reading.

Rainy Day Ideas: Make collages from old magazines and calendars. Make necklaces and different kinds of bracelets (ankle, wrist, upper arm) from a bucket of beads and a stretchy cord. These can be gifts for family, friends, pets, stuffed animals and dolls. Coloring, molding clay, chalk, painting, face painting, braiding, board games, Lincoln logs, maze books. Teach your children how to knit and sew. Make necklaces or wind chimes out of shells collected at the beach. Start a rock collection. Swim at the local YMCA or Rec center. Spend time at the library; many have programs and classes for children. Take an umbrella and walk in the rain. Find trees to climb, they're out there. Let children get dirty and wet; let them taste life! Go out at night and look at the stars. Let them run free at the beach or park and try not to hover fearfully.

Dress Up: Collect old dresses, hats, shoes, scarves, costume jewelry and make up at thrift stores. Let your sons partake also, there's no harm.

The adage that play is the work of children still stands. It has withstood the test of time. "Play" is the means through which children learn. Substituting teaching time for play time (at a young age) is counterproductive. Allow your children the richness of play and any experiences that cultivate creativity, discovery and problem solving. These are then incorporated into their way of life. Play is everything in a child's life; it is what a healthy child is all about.

When Riding In the Car: Please disconnect your vehicle's TV. You can tell stories, true or make-believe. SING. Look at a map and learn where out of state cars come from.

You can play word games, i.e. thinking of as many words as you can that start with a certain letter. Go around the car and take turns. The "In my suitcase I packed" game is fun. It goes like this: "I'm going on vacation and in my suitcase I will pack apples." The next person repeats "In my suitcase I packed apples" and adds something with the letter "B." The next person repeats the "A" & "B" words and then adds an item starting with "C." On and on through the alphabet. It is fun and helps build memory. You can also help kids learn the multiplication tables on car rides.

Please, please don't let your children use the computer and hand-held games to self-entertain. These devices are detrimental to your child's well-being and will sap their creative juices. My son has now thanked me for forbidding their use in our home.

*   *   *   *   *

Chapter Eight

Violence

Be the change you wish to see in the world.
—**Mahatma Gandhi**

*I*f you want your children to have peaceful, respectful relationships, let peace and respect reign in your home. Have rules about discussing things quietly and kindly. This was a difficult goal to achieve in our home. A technique we learned along the way was from the *Love & Logic Style of Parenting*. Since we cannot ever really make a child do anything, you tell her what **you** are going to do. This is very *powerful*. An example is, "I will discuss this with you when your voice is quiet and respectful." If something is said or done that causes an upset, a good way to handle it is to say:

"When you _____"

"I feel _____"

"I want _____"

Using "I" statements is a responsible way to express what you are feeling without attacking the other person.

Example:

"When you *do not come home on time*."

"I feel *worried*."

"I want *you to be prompt or call and let me know that you are okay*."

If you want your children to respect life, do not let them watch violent movies and play violent video games. Say "NO." Tell their friends' parents that you do not allow your child to do this and ask for their cooperation. Ask restaurants and play places to remove violent video games from their arcades. It only takes a moment and if enough parents ask and refrain from going to these places until they do, the games will be removed. Vote with your wallet.

"When you turn on the television, you run the risk of ingesting harmful things, such as violence, despair or fear. You can refuse to watch these programs and seek out things that are refreshing in nature, healing and helpful."[4]

Do not let your children play with guns. Killing is not a game and war is not okay. Redirect kids to other kinds of games. It is time children are taught that tolerance, negotiation, compromise and understanding are the responsible ways to handle conflicts. Anger and killing never resolve anything.

If you see something wrong going on, speak up and voice your opinion. *Things do not change when we are silent.* One person's voice can bring a tremendous amount of change. Let your child see you speaking out, but do it respectfully and kindly.

I think children should be shielded from seeing and hearing the news until around adolescence. They may be exposed at school or at a friend's home, but your home should be a safe haven.

My prayer is that all the warriors around the world will put down their weapons and their hearts will be filled with love and acceptance. Won't you join me?

*   *   *   *   *

Chapter Nine

Stress—The Enemy Within

Smiling relaxes the nervous system.
—Thich Nhat Hanh

$\mathcal{S}$tress is getting a lot of attention in the media these days because it wreaks havoc with our health. Life is stressful, it always has been. Raising children is stressful; the time constraints, needing to multitask, the constant demands, worry and guilt. I think it is one of the most difficult jobs there is and it is 24/7.

Children get stressed too and they feel ours. Perhaps they're in day-care away from you for long hours (which is hard on them); teachers expect a lot; there's pressure to excel in sports and music lessons. "Try to remove the pressure on your child to acquire external rewards. Help them to focus on the pure enjoyment of whatever they're doing rather than on winning a trophy"[5].

Dr. Wayne Dyer said: "Get your children out into nature as much as possible. Nature is a great reliever of anxiety for both you and your children. Make every effort to get out doors as often as possible. A walk through a city park, or through the streets of your neighborhood is a great way to relieve tension. With my own babies I have noticed that they cry much less when I take them outside. They smile a lot more on the grass than in the house on the carpet. Young children crave nature, and you can raise them to appreciate it by making every effort to instill a love, and a healthy respect, for the magnificent miracle that is in everything natural."[6]

Stress propels the body into a "fight or flight" response which can trigger migraines, lead to peptic ulcers, increased heart rate, hypertension and heart disease. It can also lead to obesity and a weakened immune system. It may even hinder a woman from conceiving.

"*Play* is nature's way of dealing with stress for children as well as adults."[7] Try to balance the time spent in school with time for your child to express herself artistically and allow time for *just* play as well.

Dr. Andrew Weil stated that, "Eliminating stress entirely is not an option. The goal is to change our reaction to it and by doing so, we protect our body."[8] He suggests **relaxation methods** and changing our habitual ways of reacting to things. *Habits can be changed.* These are his suggestions which I have modified somewhat. They can also be taught quite easily to children as well.

1. **Breathwork**: Inhale deeply and quietly through the nose, filling the chest and abdomen, to a count of six. Hold the breath for a count of six. Exhale audibly and slowly through pursed lips for as long as you can. Repeat... Do at least twice daily and especially when feeling stressed or anxious.

2. **Meditation**: (focused attention) Sit with your back straight, feet flat on the floor, eyes closed or gazing at a candle. Focus on the breath going in and out. You can also focus inwardly on a word or phrase such as "I am peace", or "I am love." Meditation helps us to be mindful and in the present moment. Fifteen to thirty minutes is ideal, but even five minutes is relaxing.

3. **Massage:** This is very relaxing. Partners can exchange massages with each other if professional ones are too expensive.

4. **Listening to soothing music**

5. **Taking a bath**

6. **Being in nature**

7. **Yoga**

8. **Laughter:** It has healing power and diffuses tension. Laugh whenever possible at how ridiculous life can be!

It is advisable to get a sufficient amount of exercise and rest; eat a healthy diet and do not keep feelings pent up; confide in those you trust. As a young mother I occationally went off for three to four hours by myself to nap, read and walk. It was very refreshing. *I encourage you to slow down your pace and not be constantly rushing from one activity to another.*

"If we concentrate on the here and now, without worrying about yesterday or tomorrow, our children will do likewise. Children live in the present and they know when we are with them physically but not mentally. By worrying about the past and the future, we lose the present and our children don't have us, even when we are around."[9]

"The best role model you can be is one who is happy, stress free and feeling good about yourself. Teach children that stress comes from the way in which we think, not from people or situations."[10] *It's what we tell ourselves.*

May you live with ease.

* * * * *

Chapter Ten

Screens

How many things I can do without!
—Socrates 469-399 BC

A high percentage of youth and adults are literally addicted to their phones, iPads and or laptops. To prevent addiction in *your* home, please, PLEASE limit time spent on screens of *all* kinds. (This includes you too, Mom and Dad.) Let's show our kids through our example that there is more to life than screens and cyber drama. I strongly urge you to allow computer use for homework *only* (especially with little ones) and to be *hyper vigilant* in knowing what your child is looking at. TV use should be doled out in small increments and video games PROHIBITED altogether in favor of creative hands-on play, outdoor play, sports, time with friends, daydreaming, etc.

You will never hear a doctor, educator or psychologist recommend surfing the web, playing video games and/or watching TV as healthy past-times. Parents tell me, almost in a whisper of embarrassment, that their children are on the computer all the time! PARENTS, TAKE CONTROL AND PUT A STOP TO IT NOW. A child should not have her own computer, and especially not in her bedroom where it will be *very* difficult to supervise.

I don't mean to be morbid, but if your child had just one more week to live, I guarantee that he wouldn't be sorry if he didn't have more screen time in his short life. He would probably bemoan not spending more time with his best friend, not playing more sports or swimming, not learning to ski or rollerblade, not having more ice cream cones on summer days, not learning to ride a horse… the list is endless. Get your child outside and *living life*. That's where the JOY is. Kids are very physical; they enjoy using their bodies and especially being outside in nature.

Daniel Goleman, author of *Emotional Intelligence: Why it Can Matter More Than IQ*, states, science has discovered that constant digital connectivity is stressful. "To the extent that technology absorbs people in virtual reality, it deadens them to those who are actually around them."

My adult son has thanked me for not letting him play video games as a child. He now sees that his childhood was enjoyable because he was very active and engaged with friends and sports. My daughter re-iterates that she "had a childhood because she didn't watch much TV, we went out and did things."

As the parent, it is your responsibility to make the house rules and to set boundaries. Legally, your child is considered an adult at age eighteen years of age and can then make his own decisions. However, I feel that as long as he is under your roof and you are supporting him, you get to make the rules and call the shots. YOU "Rule the Roost." **Be Strong. Hold to your convictions.**

I'm very concerned about the number of teens I witness crossing streets while looking at their cell phones, not to mention the number of drivers distracted by their phones as well. The combination of these two phenomena is a recipe for disaster.

"The disconnect between children and nature has ballooned to an all-time high. Our youths continue to break records in technology consumption while becoming increasingly detached from the natural world."[11] Let's put a halt to this.

*   *   *   *   *

Chapter Eleven

Discipline

No matter what the problem, love is the
answer and the greatest weapon.
—Bernie Siegel

Discipline is guidance that helps one to develop self-control and self-direction. A lot has been written on this subject. My feeling is that we need to be firm, loving and gentle when disciplining. We ALL want what we want, children and adults alike. The gentler the approach, the better we are able to hear what is being said and asked of us. Imagine your boss yelling at you. Now imagine him talking to you in a kind, respectful manner. Which way would you best be able to really hear him?

I've come to realize that the only time when yelling is acceptable is during a fire or a true emergency situation. Yelling shuts down communication and severs bonds. It causes people to separate instead of coming closer together.

Mistakes are great learning experiences. Strive to be positive and calm no matter what is happening; this helps children feel secure and unafraid. "All people (big and little) have equal claims to dignity and respect."[12] "What we do is never as important as how we do it; our tone of voice is key."[13] Let the message of love and caring come through in your voice.

All human behavior is learned, the desirable and the undesirable. Children learn to laugh, walk, jump and play as well as to whine, pout, sass and fight. They mimic, and what we *reinforce* gets repeated. *When correcting a child, address the behavior and not the child himself.* To say "You are a bad boy," attacks the child's self-worth.[14] A child is not his actions. It is best to say, "You have behaved badly and this kind of behavior will not be tolerated."[15]

As with most things, I believe the middle road is the best road; not too strict, not too lenient. Many things don't need to be set in stone; negotiating is a good skill for kids to learn, let them practice with you! Try getting the child's cooperation. If he needs to clean his room, you can say, "I'll drive you to the party when your room is clean," or "You can have a snack after you've taken the garbage out."

Family meetings work well with older children. It helps the family dynamic to openly discuss what's working well and what's not working well in your home. Encourage mutual problem-solving and the respectful airing of feelings. This is also a good time for parents to clearly communicate their changing expectations as the children are maturing. A talking stick can be used to cut down on interrupting; the person holding the stick has the floor and should be the only one speaking.

If your child is using incorrect grammar, take the time to correct her—over and over—until she learns it properly. The world respects those who speak well; that is the reality. Please don't tolerate swearing in your home, it is unnecessary and disrespectful.

Trust your intuition and instincts. If you suspect

that something negative is going on, chances are excellent that you are right. WORK TO STOP IT.

Parental Discipline: Strive to keep peace and harmony in your home. Commit to working out differences with your partner kindly, respectfully, and out of ear shot of the children.

* * * * *

Chapter Twelve

Spoiling

Your role as a parent is the highest, noblest calling you will ever have in your life.
—Dr. Phil McGraw

I believe that we do best by our children by "spoiling" them with lots of love, lots of books read to them, lots of time spent outdoors with them, time to play with their friends, some undivided attention with their parents and grandparents if possible, and lots of unstructured time for them to think their thoughts and dream their dreams.

We've all wondered, "Am I meeting my child's needs or spoiling her?" For the first three months of life, experts say it's nearly impossible to spoil a child. Infants must have their cries responded to, this teaches trust more effectively than anything else.

During the first year of life, children learn the concept of trust. We know this from Erik Erikson's research. To achieve this, "A baby must learn that he can rely on the affections and support of others, so he must have his basic needs met consistently and lovingly. These include proper nutrition, a comfortable temperature, dry diapers, adequate sleep and lots and lots of love: touching, holding and cuddling."[16] Babies are not grown-up enough or clever enough to ask for what they don't need. Attention from adults is a real need.

Babies need physical contact and most are uncomfortable without it. They will cry for lack of "contact comfort." Many parents misunderstand this and think they will spoil the child by holding her too much. "It is natural and instinctive for a small baby to be most easily content when he is being held by somebody. In many parts of the world babies are held and carried almost all the time. Grandmothers and older sisters take turns when mothers must be free."[17] I highly recommend "wearing" your baby as much as possible and while you're at it, sing, talk, and coo to her. Singing lullabies to infants stimulates the development of brain connections, particularly during the first three years of life. So sing your heart out and have fun with it.

If at all possible, use daycare as minimally as possible for children under the age of eighteen months. They need YOU.

As children get older and ask for things, as long as the request is made politely and without drama why shouldn't we say, "Yes" if it doesn't go against our better judgment? It is good for children to feel they have some influence over others. Negotiating is an excellent skill, as long as everyone involved is respected and cared about. Sometimes a compromise is needed. Let us say, for instance, that your child wants to go to the park. You can discuss it together and come up with a compromise; you get to read for a while, then you'll take Johnny to the park. This will help him understand other people's feelings, which is the root of unselfishness and the opposite of being spoiled. In my opinion, too many toys, clothes, gadgets, and possessions gives the erroneous message that we are all here to accumulate material things. That is not our purpose here on earth. Once that notion becomes instilled in a child's mind, it is difficult to erase. High school parking lots are full of brand new cars given to these first time drivers! What are we thinking?

I believe it is best for teenagers and young adults to earn the money to pay for the things they desire; cars, clothes, entertainment etc. Sacrificing and learning to budget builds character and appreciation. Doling things out on a silver platter is counterproductive and leads to feelings of entitlement.

*   *   *   *   *

Chapter Thirteen

Independence/Autonomy

Our kids need to be taught HOW to think,
not WHAT to think.
—**Margaret Mead**

$\mathscr{P}$repare kids for flight at an early age. Let them make decisions for themselves whenever possible; encourage them to be in charge of the details of their lives. Turn over the responsibilities that rightfully belong to them. I think homework is a good example, if your child is pretty responsible and self-motivated, let him be in charge of his homework.

Since young children want to do the things they see us doing—for example, cooking, gardening, doing laundry, washing dishes and changing tires—foster their interests and encourage their independence. They need to learn how to do these things and become proficient at them. Better to learn while the desire is there; when they are older they will need to know how to manage money, budget, write checks and balance a checkbook. Having a clothing and entertainment allowance will teach budgeting skills, such as how to stretch the dollar by buying items at thrift stores…,or not!

It's good to let kids decide what they want to wear and to dress themselves. Preschoolers and kindergarteners sometimes want to wear their favorite clothes all the time. It's OK; teachers understand this and you can wash the clothes at night! Some adolescents and teens may be inclined to dress provocatively due to peer pressure and ads on TV etc. *This should not be allowed.* Please teach them that this sends the wrong message and distracts others. (The emphasis on sexuality is taking us down a misguided path. If young parents can help turn this around, it would be great. Adults must be good role models and dress conservatively; sexy clothes belong in the bedroom.) Schools should be strongly encouraged to have and to *enforce* appropriate dress codes.

I encourage you to advocate for sex education at your child's school if it is not offered. Some parents don't talk to their children about sex and all children need to be informed.

If a child asks for advice, it is best not to rush in and answer too quickly. Encourage him to try to figure it out for himself first. You can say, "That's an interesting question. What do you think?" This builds confidence and he learns to trust himself. In the same vein, please don't speak for your child; respect his autonomy and let him speak for himself—even little ones—they need the practice and it boosts self-confidence.

Teach your child to take care of the earth by reducing-reusing-recycling. Try to *reduce* your desire for material things; how many pairs of shoes do you really need? *Reuse* things by donating unwanted items to thrift stores and purchasing from thrift stores. *Recycle* bottles, cans, metal, paper, plastics; whatever your city accepts. *Compost* food scraps and yard waste back into soil. All of these actions really help to prolong the life of the landfills. Plant a tree to help clean the air and provide cooling shade. Take the bus occasionally and carpool to save gasoline and build community. *Conserve water and electricity.* Turning off lights in rooms which are not being used helps combat global-warming. Kids learn by *example* way better than by what we say.

Let's be aware of actions that will adversely effect future generations. Turning engines off instead of idling for a minute or two helps reduce air pollution and global-warming. *Our great-grandchildren will also want clean air.*

If affordable, occasionally go out with your child to a restaurant or bakery. Teach her to order politely, to eat slowly, pay and tip. It's fun for everyone.

Encourage your children to follow their dreams, their passions…whatever brings them joy. They are here to live out their destinies. They are not here to be our little clones. They very well may choose a life that you never dreamed of for them. If they're happy, what more could you ask? What a huge gift to have you support their dreams. Too many people don't enjoy their jobs; I believe that is a cause of much of our society's ills.

"It's a bitter sweet road we parents travel. We start with total commitment to a small, helpless human being. Over the years we worry, plan, comfort and try to understand. We give our love, our labor, our knowledge and our experience—so that one day he or she will have the inner strength and confidence to leave us."[18]

*   *   *   *   *

Chapter Fourteen

Diet

We are what we eat.
—Michael Pollan

New research is finding that people who eat the most vegetables and fruits (usually seven to nine servings per day) are more optimistic, happy and satisfied with their lives and more creative.
—Nick Rose, PCC Nutritionist, Seattle, WA

If you have a newborn infant, it is *highly* advisable to nurse for as long as you can…even if it is only for a couple of days, a couple of weeks or a couple of months. Any amount of time is better than nothing at all. Breast feeding provides the best nutrition possible for the first six months of life and is so easy.

Try to have at least one meal together as a family every day; encourage light, pleasant conversation. Eating in front of a screen is not recommended. Eat slowly and relaxed. Chew, chew, chew your food and enjoy the experience. ☺

Try to eat *fresh* vegetables and fruits every day. Frozen is preferable to canned if fresh is unavailable or too expensive. *Green* leafy vegetables are highly recommended by nutritional experts. It is best to include all different kinds and colors of fruits and vegetables as they all contain different nutrients.

We had a rule when our kids were little: "Eat your vegetables first and then we'll serve the rest of the meal." It worked well, especially if they were really hungry! Fruit should be limited somewhat due to the sugar content, especially dried fruits. I highly recommend diluting fruit juices to reduce the amount of sugar ingested. Even better, just give kids water when they're thirsty.

Many Americans eat too much *protein*. Try to limit protein to a small portion of your meal. I highly recommend non-meat sources of protein such as grains, beans, quinoa (a complete protein), nuts, seeds and lentils. These foods don't involve injury to animals or to the earth. Growing cows for human consumption *greatly* damages the earth. There are now *many* vegetarians and vegans in America and worldwide. It is a healthy lifestyle. If you feel you must eat beef, grass-fed is the healthiest variety.

Meat is difficult to digest, and unless it is organic, it contains many unhealthy additives such as antibiotics, growth hormones, pesticides, dyes and GMOs. It is also very acidic. Health promoting foods such as fruits and vegetables are alkaline forming in the body—this helps keep our pH levels where they should be.

I also feel that it is best to avoid eating **dairy** products which are foods containing cow's milk. These include cheeses, milk, ice cream, yogurt, butter, etc. They too are acid-forming in the body. Many people cannot tolerate the sugar in cow's milk (lactose intolerance). Milk produces mucus in the body; we need some mucus to line different passages, but not more added in by our diets. If you feel that you cannot totally give up dairy, **cultured** yogurt or goat's milk products are your best choices. Humans are the only animals that continue to drink milk after weaning! Cow's milk is meant for baby cows who grow at a **much faster** rate than human babies. It is unnatural and unhealthy to drink cow's milk.

You are the role model for your children. Let them see you in control of your appetites, maintaining a healthy weight and eating healthy foods. Please buy **organic** foods if at all possible. Food is meant to sustain us, not soothe us. Don't let your desires and your taste buds control you. ***Do you eat to live or do you live to eat?***

My mother used to say, "A minute on your lips, forever on your hips!" This helped her control her weight and has helped me again and again over the years when I was tempted to nurture myself with food.

"If you do not provide junk food, kids will not have the option of eating it. Don't make food a big deal. Don't worry over every bite, kids will manipulate you by becoming fussy eaters. Try ignoring what they refuse to eat. By and large their bodies will tell them what they need."[19]

*   *   *   *   *

Chapter Fifteen

Health Is the New Wealth

When you have your health, you have everything.
—Augusten Burroughs

$\mathcal{A}$mericans are known for having some of the worst rates of heart disease, lung disease, obesity and diabetes. Food is now linked to all diseases; if we want good health, we need to be careful about what we put into our bodies.

The following are some suggestions which I want to share with you. There are *many* opinions about food and they keep changing!

Try to eat *close to nature*…that is, eating foods as closely as possible to how they came out of the ground or off of trees. In other words, unprocessed or unchanged by added sugars, artificial flavors, colors and preservatives, or having been genetically engineered.

Read the *label* on every food item you purchase. Ideally, there should be only one or two ingredients listed. If you don't recognize an ingredient as an "edible food", it is *not* food and should not go into your body.

If you can afford to buy *organic*, it is wise to spend a bit more to do so. I've always said, "I can't afford not to buy organic, my health depends on it."

Most non-organic foods are sprayed with pesticides. Pesticides are *poisons* that our bodies don't know what to do with and are stored in fat cells. They have *many* harmful effects on our bodies and should be avoided. If a label does not say "organic", the food *does* contain pesticides (unless a farm is in the process of transitioning over to organic practices).

Watch out for Genetically Modified Foods, called GMOs (Genetically Modified Organisms) or GE Foods (Genetically Engineered) and avoid them like the plague. They are not good for humans or for the earth.

- Organic food does not contain GMOs.

- For more information see the Appendix.

Refined sugar has now been defined as a **toxin** because it fits the description of a poison; that is, a substance with an inherent property that tends to destroy life or impair health. The naturally occurring sugar in fruit is fine; the same is true of honey. *Refined sugars* are white and brown sugar, agave, fructose, dextrose, high fructose corn syrup, corn syrup solids, multi-dextrin, etc. and should be avoided. These sugars are routinely added to many packaged and canned products and beverages. Americans consume huge amounts of sugar and it's taking a toll. We are increasingly unhealthy and overweight, with rises in heart conditions, diabetes, cancers, arthritis and osteoporosis. Childhood obesity has more than tripled in the last thirty years and one in three children is now overweight. ***All of which is linked to sugar consumption.*** (If you don't get in the habit of serving desserts after meals, no one will even miss them.)

Cancers and viruses feed on the sugar in our bodies and get stronger. Starve them out! We can retrain our taste buds to appreciate food in its natural state. Refined sugars are addictive; once you start eating them, it is very hard to stop. Additionally, *sugar suppresses the immune system*, making us vulnerable to illness. The immune system needs to be strong to protect against invading germs.

Please don't allow your dentist to use *amalgam* (silver) fillings. Ask for Composite Resin Fillings instead. Amalgam fillings contain 50% mercury as well as silver, tin, zinc and copper. Many experts believe that having metals in our mouths adversely affects our health and some think that these metals can cause Alzheimer's and Parkinson's. Many people are now having them removed to preserve their health. I did. Also, it is best to use toothpaste which does not contain fluoride.

Try to drink plenty of *purified water* to stay hydrated. *Avoid soft drinks*, as they pull calcium out of the bones. If using fruit juices, dilute them with water. Your urine should be pale yellow; if it is orange, you are dehydrated. I recommend a good *water filter*. In many cities, the drinking water contains pollutants that should be removed. The main ones to remove are chlorine, VOCs (volatile organic compounds), heavy metals (lead and mercury), pesticides, cysts, bacteria and fluoride.

If possible, choose your *carpeting* carefully, especially if you have babies who will be crawling on the floor. Many new carpets "outgas" toxic chemicals into the air; this can go on for years. I suggest wool or cotton rugs to avoid this situation. (See Appendix for more info on carpet outgassing.)

Avoid using *toxic chemicals* in your personal care products, household cleaners, weed-killers and for insect problems. These chemicals and pesticides harm the earth, animals and humans big time. There are now *many* non-toxic products available that are very effective. The latest thought on skin care products is: if you can't eat it, don't put it on your skin. Whatever you put on your skin goes into the body. Even some fibers from synthetic clothing get into the skin, so it is best to dress children in cotton clothing. There are many pollutants now a days that we cannot control, let's control the ones that we can.

Although there is a lot more to say about what affects our health...I think these topics are some of the most important.

Here's to your health!

* * * * *

Chapter Sixteen

Cars—Kids Behind The Wheel

There is no trusting appearances.
—**Richard Brinsley Sheridan**

*W*e all want wheels! I recommend that teens use the wheels on buses, bikes and skateboards until age eighteen. Sure, kids are *capable* of driving at sixteen, probably even twelve, but they lack the maturity to be as careful as we need them to be. They think they're invincible and many don't take the responsibility of operating a very heavy vehicle seriously.

We are ALL at risk when there are immature drivers on the road. Just because the law gives sixteen year olds permission to drive, this doesn't mean that parents must. *You* know your child; can they be trusted to drive safely and responsibly? Can they be counted on not to use their phones for calls and texting while driving? Have they kept their word about other issues? ***Please be a good role model and don't use your phone while driving.***

If you think you want your child to wait until age seventeen or eighteen to get their license, let them know this when they're much younger. If you wait too long to "drop the bomb", they may assume they're going to get their license at sixteen and then it can be very difficult to deter them. I've been there. Once they do get started, practice, practice, PRACTICE with them. It's a complex skill for them to learn.

Liberty Mutual States: A car turns into a weapon and can hurt you and others in an instant. Talk to teens about safe driving and the dangers of distractions, even seemingly innocent actions such as glancing down at the phone for directions. Start the conversation early, before he has obtained his learner's permit, and set a good example when *you are driving.*

Injury Prevention and Control: Motor Vehicle Safety
From the CDC (Center for Disease Control and Prevention)

Most at Risk:

- Males sixteen to nineteen years of age almost twice that of females.
- Teens driving with passengers: the risk increases with the number of teen passengers in the vehicle.
- Newly licensed drivers: crash risk is particularly high during the first few months of licensure.

Factors Putting Teen Drivers at Risk:

- Teens are more likely to underestimate dangerous situations or not be able to recognize hazardous situations.
- Teens more likely to speed and tailgate.
- Teens more likely to drink and drive.
- Compared to other age groups, teens have the lowest rate of seat belt usage.

Leading Causes of Teen Crashes:

- Driver inexperience
- Driving with teen passengers
- Nighttime driving
- Not using seat belts
- Distracted driving
- Drowsy driving
- Reckless driving
- Impaired driving

The risk of motor vehicle crashes is higher among sixteen to nineteen year olds than any other age group. Even though it's nice not to have to continue being the chauffeur, it would be best to put this off for a few years. Better to be safe than sorry.

* * * * *

Chapter Seventeen

Spirituality

We are not human beings having a spiritual experience, we are spiritual beings having a human experience.
—Pierre Teilhard de Chardin

Spirituality is a sensitive topic for many people. Please keep an open mind and take a breath. The following are my own thoughts; you are free to disregard them if they do not resonate with you.

Try to include a spiritual dimension in your family life, whether it is communing with nature, praying or meditating, affirming good thoughts, thanking a higher power for your blessings, attending religious services or something else entirely. Your personal views about God and religion are perfect for you. They may not be the beliefs that your children will ultimately choose. Better that they choose their own spiritual path than none at all out of rebellion. It is my belief that all paths lead to God, and it is really not so important which path is taken. *We ALL have the right to our own unique belief systems.*

We want our children to be happy, responsible, moralistic and to know God. If our children are allowed to choose their own spiritual path and with our sincere blessing, they will be at peace. Our children are not our clones. They may choose no spiritual path, and that decision may or may not stick.

I think we all want to show and teach our children what we believe, but at a certain point, when they are old enough to discern and appreciate different teachings, I think it is wise to expose them to other religions. You might take them to various houses of worship in order for them to get a taste of what other people believe. Just as you would expose your child to many different sports to see which one(s) she enjoys. Would you force your child to only play football because that is your favorite sport? Or, force your child to play the piano because you did? Choice is better in just about all manner of things.

Even if you yourself are not religious, remember that your child's soul came here to learn certain lessons. Don't close doors on her thinking about God; rather, encourage her to develop her own beliefs and inclinations as she matures. She is an arrow shooting out from your bow; let her FLY! *She is not you.* The world is a mess because of intolerance, judgment and greed. If we can see our way out of this mindset, starting in our own homes, the world will be a better place.

Please accept and respect your child's spiritual choices; it will help foster a wonderful relationship with her. There is no right or wrong in this matter; it's simply personal preference and what resonates in the heart. We are all individuals with our own road map. That is what makes life interesting. Please show keen interest in your child's road map.

We are not here on earth to accumulate material things or even knowledge. We are here on earth to discover our true inner selves and higher purpose.

We are here to be of service and to make the world a better place. To love one another and live our passions, whatever they are for each of us.

Life is the school, love is the lesson.

Namaste

*   *   *   *   *

Closing Thoughts

One of the most efficient and effective methods for stimulating a child's mental processes and performance is controlled breathing. Research shows that school children can increase their grades if they do breathing exercises prior to tests and assignments; these exercises also reduce test anxiety. They increase oxygen flow to the brain, which in turn boosts memory, concentration and problem-solving abilities. Breathe out for the same amount of time as you breathe in, to prevent dizziness and hyperventilation. Count of five. Repeat cycle five to six times. Practice with your child so it becomes a positive habit.
—Dr. Phil McGraw *Family First* p. 118.

- Are you open to learning from your children? Every person you come into contact with has something to teach you if you are receptive. It might even be, "I don't want to be like that!"

- *Please* let your child cry. It is a normal, natural release and should not bring any shame to girls or *boys*. Let them express their feelings freely and without judgment.

- Telling a child that his poopy diaper is "dirty" sends a very negative message. Diapers and bottoms are poopy, not dirty. Let us be careful what we say to young children who are innocent and trying to make sense of their world. Our bodies are beautiful and the way they function is nothing less than miraculous!

- When we volunteer at our children's school, it increases the child's understanding that school is important. It's also fun for the child and the parent.

- There is no need to push a child to start *reading*; wait until they are ready. They will let you know when that is, and then they will take off. There's no hurry.

- The power of prayer is phenomenal.

- Keep a watchful eye on your adolescent sons. They can be loners, and some become deeply troubled. You may need to intervene if they seem troubled.

- Be on your guard for *cyberbullying*. This is defined as harassment through email, social sites and texts. Bullying has serious and lasting effects, from depression and anxiety to suicide. Signs indicating a possible victim of cyberbullying may include: acting distressed after being on the internet, withdrawing from social activities or friendships, avoiding parties or not wanting to go to school, seeing grades falling, showing changes in behavior, mood, appetite or sleep patterns. You'll need to help your child immediately if she is being targeted.

- **Let's end discrimination one person at a time.** Children are naturally tolerant of other races unless *taught* differently. Encourage them to respect others—no matter their skin color, religion, culture, or sexual orientation—through your example. We *can* truly change the world for the better when we all make the effort.

Our true home is in the present moment. To live in the present moment is a miracle. The miracle is not to walk on water. The miracle is to walk on the green Earth in the present moment, to appreciate the peace and beauty that are available now. Peace is all around us—in the world and in nature—and within us—in our bodies and our spirits. Once we learn to touch this peace, we will be healed and transformed. It is not a matter of faith; it is a matter of practice. We need only to find ways to bring our body and mind back to the present moment so we can touch what is refreshing, healing and wondrous.
—Thich Nhat Hanh, *Essential Writings,* p. 19-20.

Parenting is not easy. If you have come away with a good idea or two, then this book will have been time well-spent for both of us. Be strong, thoughtful, firm and loving.

Every person you see has a mother somewhere who is *worrying* about her child. Let us treat each other's children as if they were our own and help them if needed. Quite simply, this is the answer to world peace!

People around the world are starving. Will you consider giving to a charity? Live simply so that others can simply live.

Blessings to you.

Quotes

Goals for Me
—Virginia Satir
Making Contact, 1976

I want to love you
Without clutching,

Appreciate you
Without judging,

Join you,
Without invading,

Invite you
Without demanding,

Leave you
Without guilt,

Criticize you
Without blaming,

And help you
Without insulting,

If I can have the same from you
Then we can truly meet
And enrich each other.

Memo

To: Parents
From: A Child

From *The Message International*, June 1991, p 40

1. *Don't spoil me. I know quite well that I ought not to have all I ask for. I'm only testing you.*

2. *Don't be afraid to be firm with me. I prefer it, it makes me feel secure.*

3. *Don't let me form bad habits. I have to rely on you to detect them in the early stages.*

4. *Don't make me feel smaller than I am. It only makes me behave stupidly "big".*

5. *Don't correct me in front of people if you can help it. I'll take much more notice if you talk quietly with me in private.*

6. *Don't make me feel that my mistakes are sins. It upsets my sense of values.*

7. *Don't protect me from consequences. I need to learn the painful way sometimes.*

8. *Don't be too upset when I say "I hate you". Sometimes it isn't you I hate but your power to thwart me.*

9. *Don't take too much notice of my small ailments. Sometimes they get me the attention I need.*

10. *Don't nag. If you do, I shall have to protect myself by appearing deaf.*

11. *Don't forget that I cannot explain myself as well as I should like. That is why I am not always accurate.*

12. *Don't put me off when I ask questions. If you do, you will find that I stop asking and seek my information elsewhere.*

13.. *Don't be inconsistent. That completely confuses me and makes me lose faith in you.*

14. *Don't tell me my fears are silly. They are terribly real and you can do much to reassure me if you try to understand.*

15. *Don't ever suggest that you are perfect or infallible. It gives me too great a shock when I discover that you are neither.*

16. *Don't ever think that it is beneath your dignity to apologize to me. An honest apology makes me feel surprisingly warm towards you.*

17. *Don't forget I love experimenting. I couldn't get along without it, so please put up with it.*

18. *Don't forget how quickly I am growing up. It must be very difficult for you to keep pace with me, but please do try.*

19. *Don't forget that I don't thrive without lots of love and understanding, but I don't need to tell you, do I?*

20. *Please keep yourself fit and healthy. I need you.*

The Caregiver and a
Healthy Family Discipline
—author unknown
A Healthy Caregiver

1. Regards highly the child's welfare and dignity.

2. Speaks the family's discipline regularly, clearly, and concisely.

3. Maintains a family discipline which is creative, and firm yet, flexible.

4. Understands the child as a developing, changing, and growing young person.

5. Grounds the child in a healthy, loving, and stable family.

6. Provides a discipline which includes loving benefits and consequences.

7. Establishes a fun, enjoyable, and satisfying life for the child.

8. Provides a discipline with clear boundaries and limits.

9. Gives high priority to order, integrity, and accountability.

10. Maintains a clear definition of what is healthy and unhealthy behavior.

11. Seeks out truth and is proactive rather than reactive.

12. Listens carefully to the child's thoughts and feelings.

13. Affirms the child, but confronts unhealthy behavior.

14. Sees mistakes as learning opportunities.

15. Normally supports natural consequences for unhealthy behavior.

16. Has consistent, gentle, yet firm response to unhealthy behavior.

17. Does not equate a failure with *being a failure.*

18. Follows personal principles and limitations when confronting issues.

19. Consistently communicates unconditional (*even tough*) love to the child.

20. Believes discipline is learning and living a way of life and not a punishment.

21. Uses no unhealthy discipline practices from his or her own childhood.

22. Does not employ a discipline which shames, devalues, or condemns.

23. Does not try to correct a child when agitated, anxious, or overwhelmed.

24. Provides correction in harmony with partner and certain involved others.

25. Models and teaches healthy behavior patterns.

26. Bases the family discipline upon values, love, acceptance, and respect.

27. Grounds the discipline in healthy family traditions and belief system.

28. Encourages the child to make amends when he has offended.

29. Works out the process of forgiveness carefully with the child.

30. Teaches the values of a conscious and consistent self-discipline.

More Quotes

Live as if you were to die tomorrow. Learn as if you were to live forever.
—Mahatma Gandhi

There's always room for improvement, it's the biggest room in the house.
—Louise Heath Leber

Welcome failure as an opportunity for learning.

My country is the world, and my religion is to do good.
—Thomas Paine

Life is like a mirror. Smile at it and it smiles back at you.
—Peace Pilgrim

Every time you are tempted to react in the same old way, ask if you want to be a prisoner of the past or a pioneer of the future.
—Deepak Chopra

Live as though nothing's a miracle or live as though everything is.
—Albert Einstein

Instructions for living a life: Pay attention. Be astonished, Tell about it.
—Mary Oliver

Peace is indivisible.
—Maxim Litvinlov

If you bungle raising your children I don't think whatever else you do well matters very much.
—Jacqueline Kennedy Onassis

We are not morally superior to anyone else.

Example is the best teacher.

Be your very best always.

It is more important to want what you have than to have everything you want.

One of the most important things you can do as a father is to show your children that you love their mother.

Parents teach lessons even when they think no one is watching.
—Harvey Mackay

Reach out eagerly and without fear for newer and richer experiences.
—Eleanor Roosevelt

Life today is too fast...and you don't get a chance to relax. Everyone's in a rush, they don't stop to smell the roses. Little children don't enjoy their childhoods.
—Observation from a 100 year old woman

Be true to yourself. Follow your own truth.

If you look for what's right in others, in relationships, in yourself and in life, you'll always find it.
—The Universe, tut.com

Children Learn What They Live
—Dorothy Law Nolte

If a child lives with criticism.
He learns to condemn.

If a child lives with hostility.
He learns to fight.

If a child lives with ridicule.
He learns to be shy.

If a child lives with shame.
He learns to feel guilty.

If a child lives with tolerance.
He learns to be patient.

If a child lives with encouragement.
He learns confidence.

If a child lives with praise.
He learns to appreciate.

If a child lives with fairness.
He learns justice.

If a child lives with security.
He learns to have faith.

If a child lives with approval.
He learns to like himself.

If a child lives with acceptance and friendship.
He learns to find love in the world.

Appendix

Regarding GMOs: The World Health Organization, The World Conservation Union and consumer activist groups are concerned about the following health effects: the production of new allergens, increased toxicity, decreased nutrition, and antibiotic resistance. Several animal studies indicate numerous health risks associated with genetically modified foods, including: infertility, immune problems, accelerated aging, faulty insulin regulation and changes in major organs and the gastro-intestinal system. Labeling laws are needed so that consumers know what foods contain GMOs and can avoid them. Someday GMOs will be completely outlawed.

Regarding Carpet Outgassing: New carpets can release toxic chemicals (VOCs) into the air. This is called "outgassing" and can create a serious health problem, particularly with infants. VOCs are volatile organic compounds which have a high vapor pressure at ordinary room temperature. Some are dangerous to human health or can cause harm to the environment. *We want to avoid them.* There are low-level VOC carpets and adhesives for laying carpets down. If possible, ask for carpet brands that have been tested and meet the low VOC emissions criteria for protecting your health. Typically, VOCs are not acutely toxic, but do have compounding *long-term health effects.* Other sources of VOCs are paints and coatings, lacquers, paint strippers, floor coverings, wall coverings, glues, permanent markers, furnishings, dry-cleaning chemicals, gasoline and auto exhaust, environmental tobacco smoke, adhesive removers, aerosol spray paints and most scents and odors.

Indoor Air Quality: Since many people spend much of their time indoors, long-term exposure to VOCs in the indoor environment can contribute to "sick building syndrome." Good ventilation such as opening windows frequently and air-conditioning systems are helpful in terms of reducing VOCs in the indoor environment.

For a Domestic Detoxification, avoid:

1. Formaldehyde: often found in cosmetics, faux wood furniture and conventional cleaning products.

2. Polyvinyl Chloride (PVC): found in water bottles, nylon backpacks, pipes, insulation, vinyl tiles and waterproofed products i.e. baby changing mats and mattress covers.

3. Phthalates: found in air fresheners, toys, shower curtains, vinyl flooring, detergents, food packaging, perfumes, nail polish and shampoo.

4. Chlorine: found in most conventional cleaning products, especially in bleach.

5. Hand sanitizers and other products to "sterilize" our homes. We don't need to be "sterile!" In fact, a little dirt is healthy for us.

Resources

Daily Affirmations for Parents
—Tian Dayton

Dare To Discipline
—Dr. James Dobson

Family First
—Dr. Phil McGraw

Hands Free Mama
—Rachel Macy Stafford

How to Talk So Kids Will Listen & Listen So Kids Will Talk
—Adele Faber, Elaine Mazlish

The Hurried Child—Growing Up Too Fast Too Soon
—David Elkind

Last Child in the Woods: Saving Our Children from Nature-Deficit-Disorder
—Richard Louv

Natural Cures They Don't Want You to Know About
—Kevin Trudeau

Peaceful Parent, Happy Kids – How to Stop Yelling & Start Connecting
—Dr. Laura Markham

Positive Discipline The First Three Years
—Jane Nelsen, Cheryl Erwin & Roslyn Ann Duffy

The Prophet; On Children
—Kahlil Gibran

What Do You Really Want For Your Children?
—Dr. Wayne W. Dyer

Your Baby & Child From Birth To Age Five
—Penelope Leach

Your One-Year-Old (The series goes through *Your Ten to Fourteen-Year-Old*)
—Louise Bates Ames, PhD & Frances L. Ilg, M.D.

Love and Logic
www.loveandlogic.com
800-338-4065
Serving parents & educators for over thirty years by providing simple and easy to use techniques to help us have more fun and less stress while raising responsible kids of all ages.

PET (Parent Effectiveness Training)
800-359-5915
Offers principles and practices that promote harmonious relationships between parents and their children, between children and their siblings, and between all who learn to use the PET approach to getting along with others.

PEPS (Program for Early Parent Support)
www.peps.org
206-547-8570
PEPS is a local Seattle organization that has served the King and Snohomish County areas for thirty years. PEPs offers support for parents of newborns through age three. The PEPS experience strengthens families, increases family wellness and prepares families to cope with life's stresses by creating small, thriving neighborhood based parent groups.

The Washington Toxics Coalition, Seattle, WA
www.watoxics.org
206-632-1545
For information about healthy products for the home, garden and children:

WAS (Wilderness Awareness School)
www.wildernessawareness.org
Wilderness Awareness School is a national not-for-profit environmental education organization established in 1983 and based in Duvall, WA. They cultivate understanding and appreciation of nature, community and self. Their dynamic wilderness education courses combine ancient and modern ecological wisdom, and empower people of all ages to become stewards, mentors and leaders.

Endnotes

[1] Wayne Dyer, *What Do You Really Want For Your Children?* (William Morrow and Company, 1985), 68.

[2] Dyer 44.

[3] Albert Einstein

[4] Thich Nhat Hanh, *You Are Here* (Shambhala, 2009), 19-20.

[5] Dyer 176.

[6] Dyer 189.

[7] David Elkind, *The Hurried Child* (Addison-Wesley, 1988), 200

[8] Andrew Weil, MD, *Healthy Aging* (Alfred A. Knopf, 2005), 204.

[9] Elkind 201.

[10] Dyer 172-173.

[11] *Seattle Times,* 28 March 2015.

[12] Jane Nelsen, *Positive Discipline* (Ballentine Books, 1987), 27

[13] Nelsen 22.

[14] Dyer 62.

[15] Dyer 62.

[16] Cheryl Erwin, Jane Nelsen and Roslyn Ann Duffy, *Positive Discipline the First Three Years* (Three Rivers Press, 2007), 85.

[17] Penelope Leach, *Your Baby & Child from Birth to Age Five* (Alfred A. Knopf, 1989), 88.

[18] Adele Faber and Elaine Mazlish, *How To Talk So Kids Will Listen & Listen So Kids Will Talk* (Avon Books, 1982), 152.

[19] Dyer 188.

About the Author

Jill Turnbull resides in Port Townsend, WA where she is involved in numerous volunteer activities. Prior to moving to the Olympic Peninsula Jill lived in Kirkland, WA for many years where she raised her children and advocated for healthy schools such as getting pesticides off of school grounds, and sugar out of the classroom. She is a retired RN who plans to take this book "on the road" and speak to parent groups. This is her first book. She dabbles in photography, loves to read, swim, dance, listen to music, knit and spend time with her children, friends and animals. She hopes to leave the world a better place.

* * * * *

❧ NOTES ☙

❧ NOTES ❧

❧ NOTES ☙

❧ NOTES ❧

❧ NOTES ☙

CPSIA information can be obtained
at www.ICGtesting.com
Printed in the USA
FSOW01n2221291015
12782FS

9 780986 283048